The Reindeer Herders OF THE Mackenzie Delta

GERALD T. CONATY

with Lloyd Binder

In association with the Glenbow Museum

KEY PORTER  BOOKS

National Library of Canada Cataloguing in Publication

Conaty, Gerald Thomas, 1953–
    The reindeer herders of the Mackenzie delta / Gerry Conaty.

ISBN 1-55263-229-6

1. Reindeer herders—Northwest Territories—Mackenzie River Delta—History—20th century. 2. Sami (Europeans)—Northwest Territories—Mackenzie River Delta—History—20th century. 3. Reindeer herders—Northwest Territories—Mackenzie River Delta—Biography. 4. Binder, Lloyd. I. Title.

SF401.R4C65 2003   305.8'945507193   C2003-902681-7

The Canada Council | Le Conseil des Arts
for the Arts | du Canada

ONTARIO ARTS COUNCIL
CONSEIL DES ARTS DE L'ONTARIO

The publisher gratefully acknowledges the support of the Canada Council for the Arts and the Ontario Arts Council for its publishing program.

We acknowledge the financial support of the Government of Canada through the Book Publishing Industry Development Program (BPIDP) for our publishing activities.

We acknowledge the support of the Government of Ontario through the Ontario Media Development Corporation's Ontario Book Initiative.

Key Porter Books Limited
70 The Esplanade
Toronto, Ontario
Canada M5E 1R2

www.keyporter.com

Design: Jack Steiner

Printed and bound in Canada

03 04 05 06 07 5 4 3 2 1

Contents

This book is dedicated to the indigenous peoples of the circumpolar world and their struggle to maintain their traditional ways of life.

Acknowledgments

This book would not have been possible without the kind support of many people. Otto Binder, Ellen Kristine Pulk Binder, and Lloyd Binder were extraordinarily open in sharing their lives with me. Susan Kooyman helped with the descriptions that accompany the photographs of modern reindeer herding. Mike Robinson, M.P. Hess, and Daryl Betania offered cogent comments on various versions of the text, and Janice Zawerbny of Key Porter saw the manuscript through all stages of the editing process.

I would also like to thank BP Canada Energy Company and Canadian North Airlines for their support of this book.

In 1929 the Government of Canada purchased a herd of 3,000 reindeer from the Lomen brothers of Nome, Alaska. They then began herding the animals westward to the Mackenzie River delta. The herd arrived in 1935 after a phenomenal trek across the northern wilderness.

Introduction

The Reindeer Herders of the Mackenzie Delta tells a unique story: how two families, the Pulks of Norway and the Binders of the Canadian Western Arctic, joined together in marriage. However, the marriage of Ellen Pulk to Otto Binder was much more than just a joining of two families; it was the union of two circumpolar cultures—Sami of Scandinavia and the Inuvialuit of the Western Arctic. The incentive for the marriage was true love; the union of two cultures was a result of American and Canadian government efforts to stave off a famine in the Western Arctic in the late 1920s. Their idea was a simple one: to take Sami reindeer husbandry to the Inuvialuit.

The Sami are Scandinavia's indigenous people, a reindeer-herding culture of about 51,000 people, spread over the tundra lands of Norway, Sweden, Finland, and the Kola Peninsula of Russia. Traditionally Sami have followed an annual season: reindeer calving took place between May and June; movement of the reindeer north to the Norwegian and Barents Sea coast happened between June and October; and the return of herds to interior forest lands for wintering near Sami settlements occurred from November to May. While the richness of Sami culture and its close connection to the reindeer is well understood by Scandinavians, little is known of them in the rest of the world. Some may have read about "Lapps" and "Lapland," but modern Sami do not like the use of these old Scandinavian terms. The essence of their culture is best summed up by their maxim: "What is good for the reindeer is good for Sami."

The Canadian Inuvialuit are at home in the Mackenzie Delta communities of Aklavik and Inuvik, and the Beaufort Sea communities of Paulatuk, Holman, and Sachs Harbour. They are part of the great Inuit culture that still embraces whaling, caribou hunting, and fur trapping, along with present-day participation in the oil and gas developments in the Inuvialuit Settlement Region. On June 5, 1984, they signed the Inuvialuit Final Agreement with the Government of Canada. This comprehensive land claim settlement has three goals: to preserve Inuvialuit cultural identity and values within a changing northern society; to enable the Inuvialuit to be equal and meaningful participants in the northern and national economy and society; and to protect and preserve Arctic wildlife, environment, and biological productivity. The Binder family of Inuvik are beneficiaries of the Western Arctic Claim, and their family story shows how modern land-claims negotiations set the stage for traditional pursuits, like reindeer herding, to continue.

This story traces Sami Pulks and the Inuvialuit Binders from Norway across the north Atlantic, and by train, boat, foot, and hoof to Alaska, Yukon, and the Northwest Territories. It is a circumpolar epic that proves both the power of an idea and the combined strength of northern cultures in a world of tundra, permafrost, caribou, and reindeer.

Michael P. Robinson
President and CEO
Glenbow Museum

1 The Circumpolar Homeland

If an Arctic tern flew to the top of the earth's atmosphere and looked down at the North Pole, the true expanse of the circumpolar world would be visible. A Canadian Arctic tern might first look at Canada's North and see the Yukon, the Northwest Territories, Nunavut, Nunavik (northern Quebec), and then Greenland, Iceland, Norway, Sweden, Finland, Russian Siberia, and, finally, Alaska. Often locked in ice, but flowing amongst the polar ice pack, are the Arctic Ocean, the Greenland Sea, the Norwegian Sea, and the Barents Sea. On the land far below are the traditional territories of the northern peoples: the Dene; Inuit of Greenland, Canada, and Alaska; Sami; and the many reindeer herding and maritime hunting people of northern Russia.

Circumpolar Ecology

Visitors from more southern regions often see the North as a vast expanse of beautiful and pristine landscape. Dense spruce forests give way to endless tracts of low shrubs, and stunted trees are punctuated by countless lakes, rivers, and streams. The land rises and falls in gentle, glacier-sculpted relief. In the west, spectacular mountains rise above the tundra. As travelers journey ever-northward the vegetation becomes increasingly sparse until they reach the desert of the high Arctic islands where even soil development is slower.

Geographers use many different criteria to define the circumpolar world. The lower latitudes, characterized by coniferous boreal forest that is dominated by pine, fir, and spruce, are called taiga or Subarctic. Traveling north, these trees diminish in height as the taiga merges with the tundra or Arctic.

The Arctic is the region that lies north of 66.7°N latitude. Here, there are twenty-four hours of daylight at summer solstice and twenty-four hours of darkness at winter solstice. This seasonal pattern of solar energy shapes the ecological character of the region. While this pattern of daylight is not as extreme in the Subarctic, there is still a pronounced difference in the daylight hours of summer and winter. This exaggerated availability of solar radiation is accompanied by seasonal extremes in climate. Winters are long and cold with inland temperatures plunging as low as –75°F to –130°F

The Arctic is defined by the distribution of permafrost and by the northern limits of tree growth.

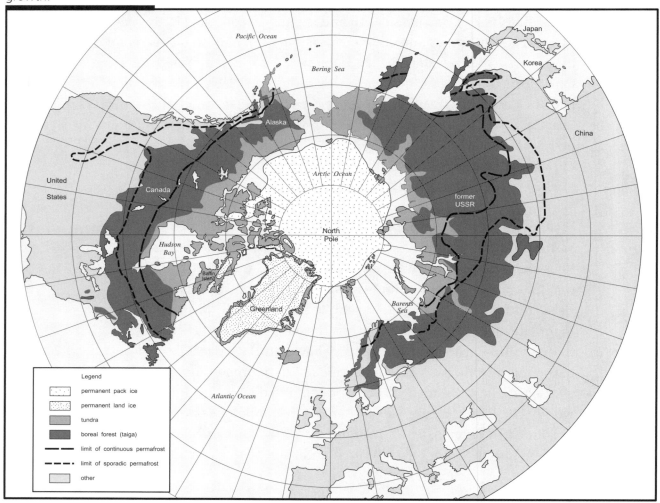

Legend

permanent pack ice

permanent land ice

tundra

boreal forest (taiga)

limit of continuous permafrost

limit of sporadic permafrost

other

(–60°C to –90°C) and –40°F to –60°F (–40°C to –75°C) near the coasts. The sparse snowfall accumulates to a significant depth during the six- to seven-month winter. Precipitation is greater in the taiga, where the shelter of the boreal forest prevents the snow from becoming hard-packed.

The circumpolar world is characterized by permafrost—ground that is permanently frozen below 4 inches (10 cm). In the tundra region, where permafrost is continuous, it may reach 1,000 feet (300 m) below the surface. The taiga has discontinuous permafrost to a much shallower depth (usually less than 325 feet (100 m). The line between continuous and discontinuous permafrost is not sharply defined, and sheltered valleys in the far north may have reduced amounts of permafrost and, consequently, greater soil development.

The length of the growing season and the amount of soil development affect the nature of the vegetation. In the Arctic tundra, plants may rise only 20 inches (50 cm) above the ground surface. Trees seldom grow to more than a couple of feet (0.6 m), except along some river valleys and near the coast of the Pacific Ocean. People are often the tallest feature on the landscape. Further south, the dense coniferous forest dominates the ecology. People are easily hidden amongst the trees.

Circumpolar Cultures

Human occupation of the circumpolar world is a relatively recent phenomenon. Prior to eight thousand years ago the entire region was covered with massive ice sheets. Some of these originated in the polar seas and spread across the land. Others formed in high alpine areas, creeping downslope until they merged with the continental glaciers. These ice masses were not static bodies, but rather grew and shrank in response to complex interactions of wind patterns, sea currents, solar energy, and other factors of which we know very little. When the ice was retreating, land became available for colonization by plants, animals, and humans. As the ice expanded, life became extinct except in areas where local geography created barriers to the glaciers. These refugia became sanctuaries where the cold-adapted life-forms survived.

We do not know why the glaciers began their last retreat. By about eight thousand years ago the large continental ice sheets had contracted to the relatively small area of our modern polar ice cap. At the same time, the mountain glaciers shrank. Gradually, the plants from the refugia spread across the newly opened landscape while other species migrated from more southerly areas. Soon, the broad sweep of the periglacial plain became differentiated into a myriad of smaller ecological communities. Before long, animals followed the plants and, over thousands of years, developed the ecosystems we know today.

While people have always been an intrinsic part of this environment, the climatic extremes of the North constrained their economic choices. The abbreviated growing season of the short summer limits plant productivity and precluded the development of agriculture. The majority of grazing and browsing animals, such as moose, deer, and elk, are solitary —except for caribou, which gather into large herds as they migrate to their spring calving grounds on the tundra and to their wintering places in the boreal forest. In the western and eastern reaches of the circumpolar seas, pods of whales cluster along their migration routes from the warmer, southern oceans. These were important sources of food for Inuit who lived in these coastal regions.

Cultures are as varied as these environments. People often lived in small groups, composed of family members, that moved frequently as they pursued the solitary big game animals or stopped where berries and other plants could be collected. Several such groups might gather in the spring and fall to take advantage of the large concentrations of caribou, geese, and other migratory animals.

The circumpolar areas lying near the Pacific Ocean are greatly influenced by the ameliorating warm currents. Here, too, whales arrive seasonally in large numbers. A large number of people are required to successfully harvest a whale, and so the pattern of settlements in the western circumpolar region was very different from elsewhere in the Arctic and Subarctic. People built semipermanent wooden structures in communities with well-defined social hierarchies. Whale meat and fish were dried and preserved for the winter months. Men who owned whaling boats commanded their crew and controlled access to food during the harshest part of the year.

The Sami of Fenno-Scandinavia differ from North American indigenous

Many different cultures have developed in the Arctic regions.

circumpolar people because they developed an economy focused on domestic animals. While linguists have drawn relationships between Sami and the ancient people of Hungary, there is archeological evidence that Sami have lived in northern Scandinavia for over four thousand years. The geography of this region is complex and Sami from different areas have found different ways of earning a living. Those who lived along the many fjords of the Norwegian coast were fishermen, known for their skills at boat building, whaling, and seal hunting. The Forest Sami inhabited the wooded valleys on the eastern slopes of the

Caribou hair is hollow and is an excellent insulator from the Arctic cold. Traditionally, Inuit made all of their winter clothing from caribou.

main mountain range where they hunted and trapped in a seminomadic annual cycle. The Eastern Sami lived near the lakes of Finland and the Kola Peninsula of Russia. Fishing was important but was supplemented by hunting and trapping. Both the Forest Sami and the Eastern Sami kept small herds (five to twenty animals) of domestic reindeer for pulling sleds and for use as decoys when hunting wild reindeer.

Among the Mountain Sami, however, reindeer assumed a paramount importance. In this region the wild reindeer migrate annually between the windblown, barren, but relatively bug-free alpine tundra and the sheltered valleys. After A.D. 1400, as other peoples continued to encroach on their land, these Sami began to rely less on wild game and more on their domestic herds. A family of five would have needed a herd of one hundred to two hundred animals. As the Mountain Sami focused on the reindeer, they changed from hunters to herders. This was a phenomenal cultural shift.

Today, people of the circumpolar world are endeavoring to maintain their traditional ways of life. This has not been easy. All of these northern people have been colonized by southern-based political economies that have tried to eradicate the Native languages, destroy indigenous belief systems, and assimilate the people into the dominant society. Moreover, a world economy has removed the people from close contact with the land and its natural resources. This contact is fundamental to the cultural identity of the people, and the maintenance of this contact and continuity with the past is essential for their future survival.

2 Reindeer Herding

Inuvialuit of the Western Arctic faced desperate times in the early 1920s. For thousands of years their ancestors relied on the sea mammals, fish, and caribou for survival. Perhaps the most important of these was the caribou. Their hollow hair is a superb insulator from the bitter cold of the long Arctic winter. Caribou hides have long been the first choice for making parkas, trousers, boots, and mitts. Caribou meat was a mainstay. Each year, as the animals congregated for their fall migration southward to protected wintering grounds, Inuvialuit hunters seized the opportunity to collect hides for new clothing and to store meat for the winter.

Caribou were an important source of food and material for clothing. A successful fall caribou hunt helped ensure survival during the long, cold winter.

The R.C.M.P. vessel *St. Roch* traveled along Canada's west coast and through the Arctic Ocean, bringing messages and supplies to police outposts and settlements in the Far North.

Inuvialuit noticed that the herds in the western Arctic were no longer behaving in a predictable way. They were no longer coming close to the growing settlements of Aklavik and Tuktoyaktuk. Hunters were being forced to travel several hundred miles to the east in search of caribou. Even then, the men had to be in the right spot at the right time to intercept the herd. It had always been a risky business. Now the odds of finding the animals were decreasing.

Also at this time the Government of Canada was expressing its sovereignty over the northern lands. The RCMP vessel *St. Roch* was launched in 1928 as a supply ship for the isolated Royal Canadian Mounted Police (RCMP) outposts throughout the Arctic. These outposts enforced Canadian law among Inuit and monitored foreign whaling and trading expeditions.

Many families still lived on the land, coming to the trading posts only when they wanted to exchange furs for tools and food such as flour, sugar, and tea. Others had begun to gather around settlements that had been established by various trading companies where they worked in a cash economy for the traders and the RCMP. The government found it easier to administer people who had settled in one place and encouraged the growth of these settlements.

The significant change in caribou migration patterns threatened the stability of the settlements in the Western Arctic. The more venturesome families left to pursue the animals, guessing where they might be intercepted. Others, who were tied more closely to the settlements, faced a future without caribou for either food or clothing.

Further west, in Alaska, reindeer—a close cousin of North American caribou—had been imported from Siberia in the final years of the nineteenth century. Native people had been urged to develop their own herds, turn from hunting to husbandry, and from an unstable to a stable, predictable resource. The Canadian government saw this as a single solution to two of their problems. First, reindeer herds would provide a constant supply of hides and meat for Inuit. Second, herding could be a means of settling Inuit in at least semi-permanent localities.

The Alaskan Reindeer Experiment

Inuit of the Western Arctic coast had, over the centuries, developed a complex culture based on whale hunting. During the ice-free season they lived in villages along the coast, from whence men set forth in umiak to harpoon beluga. Members of these whaling crews, whose members were often related to one another, and the owners of the boats held very prestigious and powerful positions in the villages. Once the water had frozen, the people relocated in more sheltered river valley settlements.

This traditional lifestyle began to change with the arrival of Europeans. Whaling ships from Europe and the United States were soon traveling to the frozen ocean. By the late 1800s the whaling industry had drastically transformed Inuit culture and had intensified to the point of threatening the survival of the very whales upon which the whalers relied. Without whales, Inuit faced starvation and extinction.

The missionaries were greatly alarmed at this situation and petitioned the United States government for assistance. Sheldon Jackson, the Alaskan Superintendent of Education, proposed that reindeer be brought from Siberia and kept at the mission stations. Sami could be hired from Scandinavia to care for the animals and to teach Inuit how to herd.

Eventually, he supposed, reindeer herding would become the mainstay of Inuit economy.

The value of the reindeer was reinforced when the discovery of gold in 1891 brought thousands of hopeful prospectors north. These newcomers had a single focus—finding and mining the precious metal. Few knew how to find food in the wilderness, and yet shipping supplies any distance in the wilderness increased the cost. Dog teams could not pull a large load. Boats were restricted by the vagaries of freeze-up and breakup of ice on the rivers. Horses were impractical in the boggy terrain. Reindeer, however, proved to be well suited for hauling freight through the forests to the mining camps.

The American program had begun in 1892 when 191 reindeer were imported to support missions in Alaska. By 1902, when the Russian Czar closed the border to export of the animals, a total of 1,200 had been brought to North America. As well, 538 animals were shipped from Norway across the Atlantic Ocean to New York. They then traveled by rail to Seattle, Washington, where they were put on a boat headed for Alaska.

Besides the herds, the Americans also brought people who knew how to care for and husband the animals. The initial shipment was accompanied by four Siberians who were later replaced by six Sami. A larger group of 118 Sami herders and their families came with the Norwegian herd. These people were to teach the Alaskan Native people how to herd and care for their animals. The government expected that, ultimately, the reindeer would be the property of the Natives, providing income and food.

The Alaskan reindeer industry quickly expanded. In the early phase, between 1892 and 1914, the herd sizes steadily increased, although ownership was concentrated with the government and the missions, with only some herds owned by Sami and Native Alaskans. Non-Native ownership increased between 1914 and 1939, as did the commercial exploitation of the herds. By 1925 there were 350,000 reindeer in 110 herds employing six hundred Inuit and several hundred Sami. Almost 200,000 of these animals were owned by non-Natives, of which 175,000 were harvested for food. This harvest was an important source of food,

Reindeer are excellent draught animals for Arctic conditions. They eat local vegetation and so, unlike dogs, do not require their feed to be transported. They are better suited than horses to both the closed forest and the open tundra. These Inuit women from Cape Prince of Wales, Alaska, are standing with their sled reindeer.

The Lomen brothers of Nome, Alaska, raised reindeer and shipped the meat to Seattle and San Francisco. Their company was successful during the 1920s but met growing opposition from the cattle industry during the 1930s Depression. The brothers were eventually forced to sell their herd.

The Lomen Brothers exported canned reindeer meat to markets in the "lower forty-eight" United States.

and the meat sales gave Inuit ready cash, thereby avoiding a complete dependency on the government. This was the model that the Canadian government wished to follow.

Others were also tempted by the commercial potential of reindeer herding. Among these were the Lomen brothers of Nome, Alaska. They purchased their first herd of 1,200 animals in 1912 and steadily increased their holdings. They also devel-

Danish biologist A.E. Porsild was hired by the Canadian government to organize the Canadian Reindeer Project's rangeland and operations. Here, he is standing outside the main building at Reindeer Station, Northwest Territories.

oped a complete infrastructure for butchering the animals, freezing the meat, and shipping the product south. Their distributors in Seattle, Portland, Minneapolis, Chicago, Oklahoma City, New York, and Boston worked hard to create a market for reindeer meat within the United States. The Lomen Reindeer Company was highly successful between 1920 and 1929.

Unfortunately, the onset of the Great Depression in 1929 had a crippling effect on their enterprise. Cattle ranchers in the American West were facing ever-lower prices for beef. They objected to the competition from Alaskan reindeer and pressured their politicians to restrict access to the market. At the same time, the brothers were facing growing opposition in Alaska to their business. Other herders claimed that the Lomen herders were unfairly encroaching on rangeland that had been traditionally set aside for communal use by Native villages. It was also alleged that, in their annual roundups, the Lomen wranglers frequently incorporated unmarked animals that belonged to other herds. Between 1929 and 1939 there were many federal investigations into the Lomen brothers' operations. Finally, in 1937, the *Reindeer Act* restricted reindeer ownership to Alaskan Native people. But by then the Lomen brothers' company had sold a substantial portion of their herd to the Canadian government.

The Canadian government had considered animal ranching in Arctic Canada as early as 1919 when a Royal Commission was appointed to study the possibility of reindeer and musk ox herding in these northern lands. The Commission's 1922 report, which recommended that herding operations be established, identified three important benefits to the development of herding operations:

- First, reindeer thrive in the harsh Arctic landscape, which is desperately short of renewable resources.

- Second, reindeer would provide meat products in an area where much of the food is imported.

- Third, reindeer maximize land utilization by creating a local resource from otherwise useless vegetation.

The Canadian Reindeer Project

In 1926 the Danish botanist A.E. Porsild and his brother Robert T. Porsild were hired to survey the western Arctic for a suitable reindeer range. They traveled eastward from the Alaska–Yukon border to the Coppermine River. Their 1928 report recommended the Mackenzie River delta as the area that was most suitable for developing ranges.

The 3,000 animals purchased from the Lomen Reindeer Corporation began their trek eastward from Kotzebue Sound at Christmas, 1929. The animals were to be guided along a route that avoided the coastline, where they would encounter Native-owned herds. Reindeer like to gather together, and it was feared the moving herd would lure animals away from the local population. Instead, a more difficult path was planned across the Brooks Range of the Rocky Mountains. This was uncharted wilderness; there were no roads and no maps. Airplanes were just beginning to appear in the north and their range was very limited. Logistical support would prove to be very difficult.

The Lomen brothers and the Canadian organizers of the operation thought that it would take, at the most, two years to complete the journey. However, the trek was troubled from the start. Bad weather, poor pastures, and a constant need to provide supplies for the herders slowed the movement as the route was constantly readjusted. Passing caribou often led away many of the reindeer, creating further delays while the animals were recovered. By the late winter of 1933 the animals and herders finally arrived on the west side of the Mackenzie Delta. Bad luck continued to follow the herd. There was little snow, and the animals refused to cross the clear, windswept ice. It was not until March 1935 that the herd could be taken safely across the ice to its new home near the settlement of Kittigazuit.

Kittigazuit is situated among a maze of low-lying islands and mud flats. It soon became apparent that this was a poor location for a reindeer herding operation. A second choice, Koryak, was seven miles upstream on the Mackenzie River from Kittigazuit, and has both unlimited pastures and easy access to the river. While the open terrain was conducive to herding, a lack of firewood made the settlement unsuitable as a headquarters for operations. Finally, a new town, Reindeer Station, was built sixty miles further upstream and became the administrative center for the Canadian Reindeer Project.

Reindeer Herding

Reindeer, like their cousins the caribou, are gregarious, migratory Arctic mammals. Each year they move to the calving grounds where the young are born. There seems to be a homing instinct, and the animals will return to the same area year after year. In mountainous regions these grounds may be above the treeline.

This is the first herd of reindeer to come to Canada as part of the Canadian Reindeer Project. Lloyd Binder's grandfather, Mikkel Pulk, helped bring this herd to the Mackenzie Delta in the early 1930s. Today, Lloyd's herd is directly descended from these animals.

In Arctic areas, the calving grounds are usually along the coast. Both environments have an abundance of green grass for grazing and willow shrubs for browsing. The open plains, and especially the coastal beaches, have sweeping winds that drive away the black clouds of flies and give the animals some relief from this constant torment.

The autumn finds the animals gathered into large herds and moving into nearby forests below the treeline. During the winter they feed mostly on lichen, a plant organism composed of fungus and algae growing together in a close association. Lichen is very fragile and very slow growing. It recovers slowly from overgrazing or trampling by excited animals. At the same time, good lichen pastures are crucial for the survival of reindeer during the long, cold winters.

The Sami of northern Europe and Asia have developed a complex culture based on the herding of reindeer. For nearly one thousand years Sami and their ancestors have

Lichen is a combination of fungus and algae, growing close together. The animals like it so much that the herders often refer to it as "reindeer candy."

Reindeer Station was built as the administrative center for the reindeer project. Access to the town's facilities was restricted to the Project's employees. This created animosity among some of the local hunters and trappers.

followed reindeer, husbanding them to improve the quality of the animals. Some individual animals have even been tamed and taught to pull sleds. The traditional Sami find that their lives are intertwined with the animals. Their cultural and personal identity is based upon a close association with reindeer.

When reindeer were brought to North America, it seemed only natural that Sami would be hired to teach the Native people here how to herd. Sami followed a practice known as "close" herding. Herds were relatively small, perhaps only two or three hundred animals. A family is able to follow the herd as it migrates and keep a constant watch over the animals. It is a very labour-intensive undertaking and requires a large investment of time and energy.

Sami who came to North America tried to teach this herding method to Inuit. However, the Canadian herd was very large—nearly three thousand animals. The "close" herding brought in very little money for each herder family. Moreover, by keeping the animals close together and their movements restricted, the forage was often in danger of being trampled. The animals were continually agitated and their body condition deteriorated.

Reindeer vs Caribou

Caribou and reindeer are both members of the genus that biologists call *Rangifer rangifer*. For that reason scientists often refer to them as being the same animal.

However, caribou have longer legs and their heads are larger and appear more square. Although they can inter-breed, caribou generally mate earlier in the fall and give birth earlier in the spring. A reindeer doe that has mated with a caribou buck will have difficulty giving birth to a long-legged calf.

Their behavior is also very different. Caribou are wild animals. They flee whenever people or dogs approach. Reindeer are domesticated and are more easily approached. Some reindeer can even be tamed and trained to pull sleds.

Sami herdsmen at a roundup in northern Scandinavia. Sami have been reindeer herders for thousands of years and the Canadian government hoped that they would be able to teach Inuit how to husband the animals.

It had always been the intention of the Canadian government to have Inuit as owners of the reindeer herds. In the late 1940s the main herd was separated into four smaller herds, each containing about nine hundred animals. By this time the Pulks were the only Sami remaining in Canada, and Mikkel Pulk became chief herder for the project. All of the herders continued to practice "close" herding, although returns were meagre. The project struggled until the mid-1960s when the smaller herds were once again brought together.

Mikkel Pulk watches reindeer as they slowly disperse while his dog, Snag, has a rest.
This photograph was taken in 1936 on the fawning grounds of Richard's Island.
Today, Mikkel's grandson, Lloyd Binder, watches his reindeer herd on this same land.

The years between the mid-1960s and the mid-1990s saw the herd
ownership transferred among several Inuit. "Close" herding was abandoned, and the government promoted "open" herding in which a range
area was selected and the animals left to browse for themselves without
being directly herded. At times, this became "free" herding as the animals became effectively wild and were corralled only at slaughter time.

Today the herd is owned by Kunnek Resources Development
Corporation. Lloyd Binder, the herd manager and part owner, is the
grandson of Mikkel Pulk, and his father, Otto Binder, was one of the first
Inuvialuit to herd reindeer. Lloyd is carrying on a tradition that has
spanned continents and centuries.

Sami of Fenno-Scandinavia are fishers, forestry workers, and reindeer herders. The Canadian government recruited some of these herders to look after the reindeer in the Mackenzie Delta and to teach Inuit how to care for the animals.

3 Otto Binder

Otto Binder first saw reindeer as they entered Canada at the end of their epic trek from Alaska. At the time he was a student attending a residential school near Shingle Point, Northwest Territories. A few years later he joined the Canadian Reindeer Project and became one of the first Inuit to own a herd. His experience reveals the frustration of merging a northern way of life with the expectations of managers who came from southern Canada.

[Lloyd] My dad is from the Tree River area. Today that settlement is called Kugluktuk, or Coppermine. His father, who was also named Otto, was German but had immigrated to the Arctic via the United States. Otto Senior had been trapping on Banks Island in the Western Arctic and, by the 1920s, had begun to work for the Hudson's Bay Company. He married Annie Taktagun, and their son, Otto Junior, was born in 1921. My grandfather was killed shortly after.

[Otto] My mother and father lived in Tree River. He worked for the Hudson's Bay Company and was in the habit of having breakfast with the local Royal Canadian Mounted Police officer, Corporal Doak. They would alternate: one day my father would go to the police station and one day Corporal Doak would come to our house. On the fateful day, it was my father's turn to visit the RCMP. Corporal Doak had two Inuit prisoners, but they did not have a real lockup. I heard later that he had been trying to scare them by threatening that they were going to be hanged. The prisoners shot the Mountie with his own rifle and then waited until they could see my father making his way across the ice, toward the

detachment. When he was about halfway, they killed him—
murdered him. He probably didn't even know what hit him.

Then the prisoners come over to our house and began banging
on the door. My mother opened it and asked "How come you're out?
You're supposed to be in the lockup." They told her that they had
just killed the policeman and my father. They began threatening my
mother, saying that they were going to kill her too. But my mother
was a very strong person. She took the gun away from them and
sent them on their way. That is why I am alive today.

[Lloyd] *Annie Taktagun then married Otto Senior's best friend, Cyril*
Wignek. They had several other children, including Helen Maksagak,
a former commissioner of the Northwest Territories and for Nunavut.
Cyril soon left the Coppermine area and moved westward to the
Mackenzie River Delta.

[Otto] *My stepfather was working for the Hudson's Bay Company*
and moved west while I was still a baby. One day they were digging
an ice house in the ground and using dynamite to create a hole.
They had gotten about ten feet (3 m) down, and my stepfather
went down to light the fuse. He slipped as he was climbing up the
ladder and the dynamite went off before he could get clear. The
explosion lifted my stepdad right out of the hole and he landed ten
or fifteen feet (3 or 5 m) away. It blew the right side of his face off
and he lost his right eye. He lived through that, although he didn't
get any compensation from the Hudson's Bay Company. In those
days they didn't have compensation for people. You got what you got.

Cyril was a skilled translator and he soon found employment
with the RCMP and with others, such as the explorer Henry Larsen.
Because we mostly lived in settlements, my life was quite different
from the people who lived a more traditional lifestyle in the
"bush." Sometimes I would accompany my father on patrols with
the RCMP. Then I would see how people lived on the land.
Sometimes I even stayed in snow houses. I enjoyed that.

The kids in the camps learned by watching the older people
and by playing games among themselves. They would pretend to

As a Royal Canadian Mounted Police Special Constable, Cyril Wignek was responsible for carrying supplies and messages by dog team. Here he is shown with the *St. Roch,* which is locked in ice for the winter, and several unidentified police officers.

make a house, and the girls would stay home to cook while the boys pretended to go hunting. That's the way they would imitate the grown-ups; that's the way they learned. They would play hide-and-seek, too. Some would pretend to be caribou while others pretended they were hunters and tried to sneak up on the caribou. That is the way they learned how to do their hunting. They would hide and see if the hunters are going to see them.

And when they got old enough, then the hunters took them out to get seals. The girls would stay at home with their mothers, learning to sew and cook. Whenever someone returned it was the girls' job to take the kamiks (seal and caribou skin boots) and dry them off and put them away. All the snow was beaten from the fur, and the kamiks were laid on a rawhide rack above the kudlik (lamp). It was important to look after the men, since they were the ones who supplied the food.

Inuit children learned life skills by helping and imitating adults. Girls spent time with their mothers, keeping the kudlik (lamp) lit, cooking, and sewing.

Children would imitate these roles in their games. They watched how old people did things and then play amongst themselves until they got to the age when they wanted to go out hunting too. And of course, the girls have to stay with their mothers. They have to learn how to watch the kudlik and how to cook. That's the way the kids learn when they are still quite young.

The children also learn by doing chores around the camp and by following the adults and watching. Their mother would tell the boys, "Watch the hunter. Watch the way your dad does it. Then when your dad tells you what to do, you know what to do." It's the same thing with the girls, they watch their mothers—how they sew

The kudlik (soaptone lamp) provided light, heat and was used to cook meat. Pieces of fur, floating in seal oil, wick the fuel to the flame. It is an important skill to know how to keep the wick trimmed and the flame burning.

and how they cook and prepare the kudlik, fixing the lamp. The adults start by teaching the children how to get ice and snow for water and how to choose the right kind of snow for water. Inuit have many names for the different types of snow—for drinking, for driving your sled, for cooking. Crystal snow is good for drinking. You can't use the snow that has drifted over, it will weaken you. But crystallized snow is like sucking ice. There is a different name for snow used to build shelters, snow that is hard to drive a sled across, snow that is easy to travel on. Snow is so important that there are many names for all the different varieties.

When you are a child you can just do so much. While you are young the adults did not push you too much. But they started children working early. It was not all play, play, play. The play

Inuit in the central Canadian Arctic spent the winter living on top of the frozen sea.
They hunted walrus and seals by finding their breathing holes and waiting patiently
for the animals to surface for air. As the prey approached the surface, the hunters
speared it and pulled it on top of the ice.

*had a purpose. The adults encouraged boys to play as if they were
going out hunting, pulling a real sled with some of the puppies.
The girls would have a small snow house where they would pretend to sew and cook. By the time a child was nine or ten they
were expected to do adult work.*

*Everyone—adults and kids—joined in the games. During the
winter they sometimes made special snow houses for playing in.
They would ice up the walls and stretch a rope across and pull on
the rope. You would think the snow house would collapse, but it is
strong. They would have the high kick and contests of strength. It
kept people fit during the coldest and darkest part of the winter
when they did not travel too much.*

*In the winter, the men hunted seals at their breathing holes.
Their dogs sniffed out the holes in the ice where seals surfaced for
air. The hunter then tested the hole with a long rod to see if the*

hole went all the way down to the water. They try not to disturb it too much. At the top, they put a little pinhole and stick a feather on a bit of ice by the opening. When the seal is coming up it moves that feather—they know that a seal is coming up—so they just spear it. That is the way they hunted seal.

They can stand there waiting, hour after hour. Often there are a lot of seal holes, some of them quite a distance from the others. They wait and wait and wait until finally one seal comes up. If there are too many holes and there are two or three guys hunting, some of the hunters close the more distant holes by putting ice blocks into the breathing hole. If there are too many breathing holes you will never get your seal. You have to wait until the seal comes to your breathing hole. You have to have a lot of patience for that.

And when they are waiting beside the seal hole they have a little square piece of caribou skin. When you walk on snow you hear that crunch, crunch, crunch. When they are beside the seal hole, they have that little piece of caribou skin to stand on. Sometimes they wait three or four hours for the seal to come up. That is a tough life. Some still hunt that way, although no one does it full-time anymore.

But everything changed once the missions started taking over. During the 1920s and 1930s the children were taken from their families and sent away to hostels.

[Lloyd] My dad was sent to a residential school at an early age.

[Otto] I was about seven or eight years old when they sent me to school at Shingle Point, Alaska. Inuit were starting to change our way of life, to live more in the settlements and less on the land. My generation was one of the first to be sent to the mission schools. I was at the school at Shingle Point for six years. During that time I never saw my mother or father because they had no way of traveling from the Eastern Arctic to the west. When I finally went home I almost did not know my parents. I was at Tuktoyaktuk then. I came out of school from Aklavik the last year.

I knew my parents were coming west, they were coming to "Tuk," and I arranged to go there on the mission boat. The mission boat took all the children who were going home, and there was a large group of us on it at that time. The church officials let us stay at the mission in "Tuk" until our parents arrived. I almost did not know my mother! That's why, when I was working with the reindeer and my own children were getting old enough to go to school, I decided to move to town. I did not want them to have the same problem that I had. I did not want them to forget me. It is important to know your parents.

[Lloyd] Times were pretty tough when my father returned home. Within a few years he was on his own.

[Otto] I had nine stepbrothers and stepsisters in total, I guess. Cyril was getting pretty old and was not too well. The injuries from the dynamiting accident really began to affect him. By the time I was seventeen years old, I was doing a man's work. I would have liked to have played, but by the time I was finished all my chores, I was too tired. I was also working part-time for the Hudson's Bay Company.

My best friend, Jimmy Jacobson, was in a similar situation. One day we decided to head out on our own. I left my wages for the year—about three hundred dollars—for my father. We bought some ammunition, flour, tea and sugar, and cheese and hitched up a couple of dog teams and left home. We were going to live off the land. It was springtime and there were lots of ptarmigan. We shot these, but we were not very good marksmen and used up a lot of shells. Actually, you cannot starve on the land. You might go hungry some days, but you will not starve if you know what you are doing.

We traveled up to Bailey Island, where the ocean opens up. Seals come in there and we had lots of food for ourselves and our dogs. We did not build snow houses. Instead, we moved into log houses that other people had built and abandoned.

Logs came down the Mackenzie River, drifted out to the ocean and spread out all along the coast. In some places, where there are lots of these logs, people built houses with them. We stayed out a couple of years. I never became a very good trapper, though. I had been going out with good trappers, following them around just for company when I was younger. In those days trappers made good money. But I never got to like trapping. I did not like skinning the animals. When you are very young, that is the time to learn. And mostly it is the women's job to skin the animal. But I had not learned how to do that and at the time I was single without a wife to help me. So we gave it up after a while.

[Lloyd] *After trapping for a few years, my dad returned to Tuktoyaktuk, looking for work. He was hired as an apprentice reindeer herder.*

[Otto] *I was nineteen or twenty years old when Jimmy and I came back from Bailey Island. I'd seen the reindeer herd when I was a student at Shingle Point in Alaska. In 1932 they came while we were in school. Mr. Crawley, the manager for the Lomen brothers, and some of the Lapp herders came into town. They told our*

Otto Binder and the other herders kept track of the reindeer by patrolling on skis. They often skied 20 or 30 miles (30 to 50 km) each day, counting the animals and keeping predators away.

The herders stayed with the reindeer 24 hours a day. Winter shelters, such as this, were built of sod and logs. Shown in this 1934 photograph are (left to right) Louis Brockage, Mrs. A.E. Porsild, and Mathias Hatta.

school principal that the reindeer are up on top of the hill. So they gave us one day off to look at the herd. I met Mr. Crawley and Andrew Bahr, the chief herder for the reindeer trek. I got quite interested in them. We saw the reindeer in harnesses, pulling sleds. Some of the herders were skiing, too. The animals were so tame, they let us pet them. I liked them and remember thinking, "Some day, when I get old enough, I'd like to work with the reindeer." So,

Charley Rufus is holding a reindeer fawn in the corral on Nicholson Island, Northwest Territories. By the late 1940s the government had begun turning the reindeer over to Inuit herders.

when I returned from Bailey Island I took a job as an apprentice herder.

Herding was a different lifestyle than anything I had done before. They are four-legged animals and they are always moving. You really have to be on your toes to keep track of them. It's not so hard in the winter time when you can follow their tracks in the snow. I used to ski 20 or 30 miles (30 or 50 km) in a day, watching over the herd. The spring and summer are the most difficult times to herd. As soon as the snow starts to go, they smell fresh green coming up somewhere and they are gone.

Before we had our own herd the government herd was up to seven thousand animals. There were fourteen herders. One time, when they were rutting, we counted all seven thousand animals. On our next count, a few days later, we were down to four thousand! That's three thousand gone! Somewhere! People were seeing them in Coppermine. People were seeing them in Yellowknife. They had drifted off with the caribou. That's what can happen when the herder isn't paying close enough attention.

I had a lot to learn about herding. Once, when I was just beginning, I was told to bring the herd down to the post. It was a trip that should have taken two days. But we were young and thought we would show everyone how hard we could work and what good herders we were. We did the whole trek in a single day. We thought we had done a great job and would be praised by the boss. Instead, he really tore a strip off of us. We had driven the herd too hard. The does were close to fawning and we had pushed them too fast. After that, they always sent an older herder to hold us young guys back.

We were with the reindeer twenty-four hours a day. Each herder would work a twelve-hour shift. The reindeer became very accustomed to people. Sometimes they would graze way out, and we would have a herder's tent on top of a hill to keep an eye on them. When the wolves started chasing the reindeer they would come right over to the tent and start milling around. The reindeer knew the herders would get the wolves. And the wolves could smell us. Usually the wolves would leave the area. Those reindeer knew where it was safe.

[Lloyd] *While he was an apprentice herder, my father married Ellen Pulk, the daughter of Mikkel Pulk who had come from Norway to teach Inuit how to herd the reindeer. Mikkel eventually became the chief herder. The government plan was to privatize the entire herd to Inuvialuit owners and have them run their own herds as businesses. So the original herd was split into five herds. My father owned one of these with a partner. Unfortunately, they were allocated a range fairly far to the south. This was good for the winter, but they were not given a summer range on the coast.*

Reindeer hides were collected at Reindeer Station and sent away for tanning.

[Otto] They gave us nine hundred reindeer and an area around the Eskimo Lakes as our range. Wintertime was easy. There was good terrain and good feeding grounds. But when spring and summer came, conditions became much worse. There were no beaches and nowhere to cool off. The mosquitoes and other insects were terrible. The first summer we lost around three hundred animals. We could only watch as they took off for the coast where the breeze would cool them off and blow away some of the insects. We knew they were suffering. We were suffering ourselves from all that heat. It was almost 85°F (30°C) and there was no breeze in the closed forest.

We used to try to round up strays. But we would get tired and fall asleep on a sand spit in all the heat. A bear might come along and step over us. That is how exhausted we were from the heat. But the bears were harmless. They had too much to eat with all the fawns and berries.

Many of the reindeer died. You could smell the rotting carcasses all over. But we were powerless without the government's permission to move our herd to the coast. We were not allowed to use our own judgment about where to move the herd.

After three years we were finally allowed to take our herd to the coast. But by then we had lost our heart for it. We swam our herd across to Richard's Island that summer and turned it back to the government.

We were very sad to give up the herd and our life as reindeer herders.

[Lloyd] *My dad's first job after moving back to Aklavik was with the game wardens, looking after their dogs, guiding them on patrol, and interpreting for them.*

[Otto] *When I applied for a job with the game wardens I really did not know the country very well at all. The game warden wanted someone who knew the Mackenzie Delta well so that he could travel on patrols. I told them I knew the land, even though I had not traveled through it very much. And I got the job! The first trip I got sent on was to Fort McPherson. Of course I really did not know where Fort McPherson was or how to get there from Aklavik.*

Many of the Inuit who Otto met on his patrols for the game wardens lived a very traditional life. Children would be told stories which the adults illustrated by making figures from string.

The Canadian government began to establish its sovereignty in the Arctic during the early years of the twentieth century. The Royal Canadian Mounted Police set up outposts throughout the North where they could monitor foreign whaling and trading activities and keep watch on Inuit. Often, the police officers had very little knowledge of Inuit culture.

In addition to being threatened with hanging, the two men who shot Corporal Doak and Otto Binder had been forced to sew clothes for the policeman. Among Inuit, sewing was considered women's work and this forced labor was an unbearable insult. Inuit custom dictated that a person's self-respect could be restored only by killing the person who initiated the insult.

Law officials had previously allowed Inuit revenge killings to occur without harsh punishment. With the death of the policeman and the trader, officials felt that stronger measures were needed to "educate" Inuit. The men were apprehended, tried, and found guilty. They were sentenced to death and hanged at Herschel Island.

Otto Binder's mother was Copper Inuit. After his father was killed, she married Cyril Wignek, who became a Special Constable with the RCMP. Here, he is wearing the jodhpurs that were part of his working uniform in 1929.

Otto Binder, still herding at eighty, checks the reindeer herd in March 2002. He does not miss his days herding on skis and foot. He says he can't sleep in a tent anymore, as he gets too cold and stiff.

So I walked around town, trying to meet some of the old-timers. Whenever I met one of these trappers I would talk to them and ask "Which way is the trail to McPherson? What river do you follow?" I would remember what they told me. Once you get the map in your head you can break your own trails. From then on it was easy.

But it was hard working for the game wardens. They were new to the country. There had never been game wardens or game laws. It was hard to go on patrol, trying to catch someone poaching or breaking other laws that had been made in the south. My own people thought I was working against them. I worked for them for three years.

[Lloyd] *When a position as special constable with the Royal Canadian Mounted Police became available, Otto was very eager to get it.*

Otto Binder moved his family to Aklavik in the late 1950s where he worked, first with the game wardens and then as a Special Constable with the RCMP. They left the tent dwellings of the reindeer camp for a small, wooden house.

[Otto] I saw my game warden boss and the RCMP officer on the street, and he said they were looking for a special constable. I stood behind the game warden and started pointing at myself. I was ready to start right then! But I gave my two weeks notice before I started with the RCMP.

I did a lot of traveling by dog team for the RCMP. We went all over the Western Arctic. One year I traveled over 3,000 miles (4,800 km) by dog team. At the time, there were no telephones or other means of communication. We would be out three or four weeks at a time. Your family did not know when to expect to see you. They did not know where you were all the time. In those days, with the dog team, you could be lost for a week. No one would

Cows and calves moving free through the exit corral to find their grazing company for a summer on the tundra.

know until you got back home. A lot of time the Mounties must have suffered the cold. They had fur clothing to wear, but they were not used to it like we were.

I was pretty much my own boss with the RCMP. I would look after the dogs when we were in town and act as guide and interpreter on patrol. When I first started, they wanted me to feed the dogs every day at five o'clock. I asked them, "Why feed them at five o'clock?" When I traveled I would feed them at ten or eleven *o'clock at night. When we traveled we did not stop every eight hours. We would stay on the trail longer, depending on the weather. We might travel longer hours whenever the weather and trail were good. Sometimes we would keep going until ten or eleven at night. I liked to feed my dogs late at night to have them ready for the next day. If you feed them in the morning, they do not seem to work very hard. The RCMP let me change the feeding schedule and adapt to my own way of working. I generally had my own hours. Sometimes I would put in fifteen or sixteen hours a day.*

It was also my job to provide food for the dogs. I used to hunt whales and, in the fall, go fishing. I would set fifteen or twenty nets in the ocean and back into the river just before freeze-up. I used to catch ten thousand fish in September. I would set the net three or four times each day. By the time I cleaned out a net I would have four hundred or five hundred fish each day. When I retired from the RCMP I swore that I would never set a net again.

We moved to Inuvik after a few years. The school was better there. I was still working for the RCMP, but they had cut down on the patrols. They put me on guard duty, watching prisoners. I did not like that as much, it really was not my style. I like to travel. The job in Inuvik had me in the office most of the time. So, I finished my last five years and retired from the force.

[Lloyd] There was a big celebration in Inuvik for Otto's eightieth birthday in 2001. The officer in command of "G" Division presented Otto with a full red serge uniform in recognition of his years of service to the RCMP. It was a very emotional event.

[Otto] After I left the RCMP I began to work on the freight barges in the Mackenzie River Delta. I know the channels very well and would take small loads on my outfit. Several times the larger companies asked me to come and work for them as a pilot or captain. But I preferred to work on my own.

These days I am mostly retired, although I like to help my son Lloyd with his reindeer operation. Last winter I spent three months with them, putting 1,500 miles (2,400 km) on a snowmobile. It is so easy these days with a snowmobile. When I was younger we herded on foot, skiing 20 to 30 miles (30 to 50 km) a day. To this day, I still enjoy working with the reindeer.

Right now the reindeer are a little bit wild because they have not been herded for over forty years. Last year they got quite tame because I worked with them every day. I would get quite close with the snowmobile. They get used to you when you are around them so much and even seem to know who the person is on the snow-mobile. I guess everybody drives with their own different style. It may take two or three years for them to get really tame again. I hope I can continue to help.

In 2002 the Binder family gathered to celebrate Ellen and Otto's sixtieth wedding anniversary. The sons all dressed in traditional Sami tunics and the daughters wore dresses decorated with Mackenzie Delta braid, reflecting their cultural heritages.

Gathering reindeer in late June is often dusty and the air is full of shed hair.

Between November and March the reindeer graze on lichens. Lloyd and his herders check the herd daily to keep predators away. If no animals have strayed and if there is no fresh snow to cover up the tracks of strays, they merely drive their snowmobiles around the herd—a circle of 1.2 miles (2 km) diameter. On short days in December, they may have two hours of twilight as the best working light. If the herders encounter wolves or wolverines they chase them away and advise trappers.

About two months old, this reindeer fawn shows off his new ear tag. All new animals are ear tagged with plastic, numbered tags. Each year a different color is used, which allows the herders to quickly estimate an animal's age.

Roundup and handling is very busy as many animals are handled as quickly as possible. Here, Lloyd's son, Kristian, holds a fawn while Lloyd places an ear tag identifying it as a reindeer, and for health monitoring.

Lloyd's sister, Ingrid, struggles to hold a fawn for tagging and treatment at the 1999 roundup while he watches. His siblings often help at roundup, as do visitors.

Today, reindeer herders travel by snowmobile, not skis, in the winter. Otto Binder (standing) and Sandra Burns (Lloyd's companion) check the herd.

Plant life is fragile in the Arctic. Herders must be careful that they do not over-graze the land nor let the reindeer get excited and trample the plants.

A major roundup activity is to collect velvet antler from reindeer, which is processed for the health food industry. A veterinarian takes blood samples to monitor herd health and advise us on safe, humane, and healthy treatment of the animals. Reindeer antlers are at their prime in late June.

Today, the Sami continue to wear a distinctive style of clothing, although usually only on formal occasions. This suit was worn at a wedding and features a hat with four extensions which represent the four directions of the wind.

4 Ellen Kristine Pulk Binder

Ellen Kristine Pulk Binder is the daughter of Mikkel and Anna Pulk, two Samis who came to Canada in the 1930s to teach reindeer herding to Inuit. She married Otto Binder and together they raised a family while trying to keep their reindeer herd. The failure of the herd and their move to Aklavik was a very sad occasion. Ellen speaks frankly of life in the then-newly established northern settlements and reflects on some reasons for the reindeer experiment's failure.

[Lloyd] My mother, Ellen Kristine, is the daughter of Mikkel and Anna Pulk. Mikkel came to Canada in 1931 to teach reindeer herding to Inuvialuit in the Western Arctic region, in the Mackenzie River Delta. They came from Finland with my mother, who was six months old, and their son Nils, who was about two years old. They were one of four Sami families contracted by the Canadian Reindeer Project.

[Ellen] My parents were recruited by the Canadian government in 1931 to teach reindeer herding to Inuit. The Porsild brothers had a great deal of difficulty recruiting Sami for the Canadians. Many had never been beyond their own country and had no inclination to immigrate. Aslak, the eldest, had worked previously with reindeer, as had Mathers Hetta. Mikkel was working at the time for the Hettas, who were shopkeepers, in Kautokeino. Mikkel helped to keep books and was working as a reindeer drover when his boss made trips over the mountains. On these journeys they traveled to the coastal town of Alta and brought meat and skins to market at the spring fair in Bassekap. They returned to Kautokeino with essentials such as flour, salt, butter, and other goods for sale in the shop.

Mikkel Nilsen Pulk (left) and other Sami herders on their arrival in Canada in 1931.
Ellen is in the arms of her mother, Anna.

They traveled with a lead sled-deer and seventy-three or more reindeer tied single file, each with its pulka (sled) loaded. The trip sometimes took several days owing to inclement weather over the mountains. Mikkel did not own his own reindeer, nor did his family own any.

It was hard to leave their homeland and come to Canada. But times were tough in the 1920s and 1930s. My mother, Anna, always maintained that they may not have come at all had it not been for their six-month sojourn to Germany in 1930. Anna and Mikkel, with sons Isak and Nils, were with a group of thirty-two Sami and thirty-two reindeer who traveled to Germany in 1930 as a sort of circus group to show Sami lifestyle and culture in Berlin and Munich.

After returning to Norway they met Bob and Erling Porsild, who had been sent to recruit potential herders as trainers for Inuit and the reindeer herd that was en route from Alaska to Canada. Mikkel yearned for a freer life on the land and had no prospects of becoming a herd owner. The trip excited my parents' interest in seeing other countries and they felt that it might offer a better life for themselves and their children.

Along with my parents, my brother and myself, there were Aslak Tormensis with his wife Susanna and their daughter Anna, who was five years old. Mathias Hetta also wanted to go, but he was single and the Canadian government would hire only married men. Mathias quickly arranged to marry Berit Inga, although she was quite young and at first reluctant. Their daughter Ellen Drislind was born just prior to departure and was only two old when they finally arrived in the Mackenzie Delta.

The emotional leave-taking from family in Kautokeino was stressful. They took a river boat to Galanito, where the goods and children were loaded on sleighs pulled by horses. The adults walked overland to Finland. They then followed along the river, being careful to camp only on the Finnish side. If they crossed over to the Swedish side, they were careful to return by night. Such were the politics of the time.

The three Sami families eventually arrived in Kiruna, the largest settlement in northern Sweden. They then took the train to Gothenburg and boarded the SS Gripholm to cross the Atlantic Ocean. They arrived in Halifax in July and, after several days, were brought to the RCMP training grounds at Rockcliffe, near Ottawa.

The Porsilds had told us to bring only the most necessary items. At Rockcliffe we were issued extra clothing, cooking utensils, and a very minimum of other items. We then left by train for the long journey to Athabasca, Alberta. There we changed to a scow and began the trip down the Athabasca River and Mackenzie River. It took us three weeks to reach Aklavik.

Aklavik was a small fur-trading post at the time. There were buildings for the RCMP, the wireless crew, two mission churches

In the early days, herders walked a lot, and herding dogs could save work. Mikkel Pulk (center) with other herders pause during a roundup. A breed of collie dog was often used, and still is today, to herd reindeer.

with their own staff, a doctor's residence, and a few cabins of Gwich'in. Inuit and Gwich'in came to the village only for trade.

What desolation for us! But us children adapted. We were playing with Inuit children, having a great time. But I remember my mother waiting for news from home. But all of the letters were censored. By this time the Nazis had invaded our homeland and all the mail was censored. Why would they censor Samigiella, our language? The people were only getting literate then and starting to write Samigiella. Who would they have gotten to censor the letters? It all seemed very unfair to us.

My father kept renewing his contract. He started as a regular herder and soon became the chief herder, a position he held for twenty-five years. He retired in the 1960s when the Canadian government retired the Canadian Reindeer Program and turned the animals and other assets over to another branch of the government and, eventually, to the Canadian Wildlife Service. Contract managers were hired to run the program, and it became a lot more controlled by the urges, whims, and desires of the managers rather than a direct government program. So Mikkel retired and returned to Norway. He was awarded the Commissioner's Medal for the Northwest Territories and returned for those ceremonies. He died in 1994 on a visit to Canada.

[Lloyd] *My mother found that life for a girl in Canada was much more restrictive than it would have been in Norway.*

[Ellen] *That was something else I found out when I brought my father back to Lapland. If I had been living there I would have been allowed more freedom rather than being told to work all the time. There, the girls were allowed to laugh and play. We were not permitted to do that.*

I would cry because I wanted to play but my mother would say, "You might as well learn. It's going to be part of your life. You might as well learn now. You're my only daughter." And work in camp! It means making bannock (a biscuit-bread that is a staple food among northerners). It means keeping the stove. It means keeping the men's clothing in shape so it won't wear out.

You are moving a lot. But during the day you are confined to a small area around the camp. I could not even borrow my brother's skis because we had only one pair of skis issued to us. So I did not even have the satisfaction of going skiing on my free time. It was a freedom thing, but I did not know. I could not complain too much. Still, I look back and think what it would have been like had I been in Lapland. I might have had more freedom.

[Lloyd] *Still, the reindeer project did offer some benefits.*

At first Sami herders were under the direction of government supervisors. Here, W.E. Hogan, the assistant foreman, visits herders Illesiak, Pulk, Cogillak, and Lulkas in the field. Such visits were often brief and did not give the foreman the opportunity to learn about reindeer herding. As a result, poor decisions were often made about the herd.

[Ellen] So, this program was intended to provide meat for Inuit. Perhaps in the long run it may not have succeeded, but it helped a lot of people in our area adapt to a changing lifestyle. In the camps you were issued rations. When the herders first came to camp they had a hard time making it stretch because they were not being so careful and they would run out of butter, run out of sugar, and run out of flour. They learned that. And they learned to count. At least to while away the long winter storms some of them would use Monopoly. It is quite a game. And, of course, everyone played cribbage. And then they learned to handle their money more carefully, even though they never saw their paycheck. It went into the commissary. Still, they learned to know that they had so much

*money. And when they came to a community—any community—
they were the ones who settled the easiest into it. So, as a make-
work program, it was a success.*

*[Lloyd] Otto and Ellen were married and took over part of the reindeer
herd. Government officials insisted that they keep their herd in the
Eskimo Lakes area all year. Without a seasonal migration to the coast,
the animals began to die. Eventually Mom and Dad returned their
herd to the government. The failure of their enterprise and the move to
Aklavik are bitter memories for my mother.*

*[Ellen] No Inuit live inland in the summer. Nor do any animals.
Ottawa wanted to try it out. Even after the first summer they knew
it was a bad idea, but they kept to it year after year. How on earth
did someone think you could keep reindeer inland where there
were no beaches, no place for the deer to get away from the mosquitoes? And they were thick there. There was lots of water around.
You could smell the rotting carcasses all over. It was a peculiar situation. And they allowed that to go on for three years. Finally, we
gave up and moved to Aklavik.*

*Shall I give you an idea of how we moved back to Aklavik? This
was in March of the year. We sold the herd back to the government
for one dollar. We were allowed to stay in camp for three days
before we were told we had to leave. Otto had his own dog team
then that we used at Eskimo Lakes. We had a 16 foot (5 m) toboggan and we had a canvas carryall for that, you know, the
carryall that we latched down. And in that we had everything we
owned. I'll tell you what we had on that toboggan. We had the dog
pack, the cooking dog pot, a length of dog chain, as well as individual chains that were attached to that, and then we had all our
bedding, all our pots and pans, all our clothing. We put our children in the toboggan and headed for Aklavik. We camped halfway
between Reindeer Station and Aklavik. Then, we went down to
Aklavik.*

*My mother had a feeling of things that might happen in the
future. The previous year she said there was a shack for sale in*

Reindeer Station was established as the base for the Canadian Reindeer Project and was a thriving community from the 1940s to the 1960s. When the Project was privatized in the 1960s, Station was officially closed. Lloyd was born here in 1952 and often returns to visit and pick berries.

Aklavik. It was a two-room shack that somebody wanted to sell and she told my father, "Buy that shack." It was between the two missions at the back of the village, near a lake.

So we had a place to go to. We drove into Aklavik. I had been in school there and so had my brother. I had good, strong memories of heading back to the Anglican Church and the Anglican Mission and hospital where the lake was.

I saw all those cabins and I thought to myself, "How ... how am I ever going to live amongst 340 people when our biggest camp was only 50 people at the most? How will I stand a place that big?"

It was a frightening experience.

That little house looked so big. I was used to living in a tent all year. The tent was 10 feet by 12 feet (3 m by 3.6 m) in the summer. In the winter we erected a second tent inside and our living space shrunk to 9 feet by 11 feet (2.7 m by 3.3 m).

And the loss of our reindeer meant a great deal. As Sami, our lives are really intertwined with the animals. They are a part of everything. I was visiting Norway a few years ago and saw many Sami heading for the hills. Some were on snowmobiles with sleds, others were giving rides to tourists. A Sami sitting beside me said, "Look out the window. There go the real Sami." I looked at her and said, "What do you mean by the 'real Sami?' They are just as real as the rest." But you are not considered to be a real Sami unless you have some connection with reindeer. That was a big part of having to give up one lifestyle for another. That was one of the most difficult things about moving to Aklavik.

[Lloyd] *Life in the settlement proved very difficult. Otto's first job, with the game wardens, was very difficult for the family.*

[Ellen] *We were in a little two-room shack; it was insulated with sawdust and had no other insulation or board on the outside. Inside there was only beaverboard or wallpaper. A tent would have been more substantial. There was one wood-burning stove, and it took a lot of sawing to keep the stove going in the winter.*

One day we were running short of wood. The game wardens had a shed where they kept their dogs and that was where Otto would spend his day, fixing dog food, from eight o'clock in the morning until four o'clock in the afternoon. It was getting colder and colder as winter grew on. One day Otto decided that, since he had finished his work early he would come home and help get some wood in before dark. It seemed like a very sensible idea. And he did that.

The next day all of the game wardens said they did not notice him in the office yesterday and that he would find that the chief warden wanted to speak to him. The chief warden told Otto, "I

In the 1950s at Reindeer Station recreational activities were often simple, spontaneous, and brief. Young women did not have much free time; they would usually be at home sewing and cooking. Here the girls play at Maypole.

went to see you at the shed where the dogs are and you weren't there." Otto replied, "Well, I went home to get some wood in. We were running short of wood and my wife can't get the wood in with the kids." And the warden said, "Otto, we hired you to look after the dogs and take us on patrol. You work eight to four. If there's nothing for you to do there but sit and smoke, you stay there anyways because that's why we hired you."

When Otto came home I could see that he was very upset. He said to me, "You know, I don't know how long I can last at this job. I'm not supposed to come and see our home because I'm

Meat production has supplied local markets as well as markets in southern Canada. The slaughterhouse at Reindeer Station in the 1950s and 1960s processed several hundred animals over a two week period. Lloyd is planning to use a mobile plant for processing.

supposed to stay in that shed." It was a bad job. He could not go hunting caribou because the game wardens were afraid someone would say he was breaking the law. So, we were eating bully beef. Thank goodness the "specials" job opened up.

[Lloyd] Ellen watched the development of new settlements in the Arctic. She saw a great loss of the sense of community in these new developments.

Languages—New and Old

When Mikkel Pulk came to Canada he could neither speak nor write English. He had learned to read the Bible in his native Sami language, Samigiella, and began to work his way through an English version, translating word for word between the two languages. It was the only way he could compare and get a gist of the meaning of the English words. His early journal-keeping reflects this very biblical English. Over time, there is an evolution from the biblical to more and more colloquial English.

Sami language has changed greatly since Mikkel and Anna came to Canada in the 1930s. When Mikkel returned to Norway in the late 1960s, his use of the language was consider to be antiquated. A linguist from the University of Tromso interviewed Mikkel and recorded his use of archaic language forms.

Fifty years ago Sami lived a more traditional lifestyle. Both their lives and their language has changed. Mikkel Pulk discovered that he spoke an older form of Samigiella than most of the people do today.

[Ellen] *If I had not lived here I could not believe the rapid change of lifestyle. People began living in communities rather than staying in camps. People moved to the new town of Inuvik from Aklavik, and younger people began to give up trapping. It changed the whole lifestyle and you lost this feeling of community that you had in every small town. There was more contact between villages then. The government wanted to settle everything. Rather than building cabins for people and giving them rations to stay in the camps, they encouraged everybody to move to town. It changed the whole life system.*

The way Inuvik was constructed contributed to the loss of a sense of community. This town was designed in southern Canada. They built a "utilidor" to carry all the water, waste, gas, and power in a heated conduit above ground. At Aklavik they had found these things froze in the ground during the winter. Well, the serviced area of Inuvik had the schools, the hospital, the apartments for the people being serviced in the town (the bigwigs and whatever). And then they built the area where they were encouraging people to move to from Aklavik. This area was unserviced. We were still using "honey buckets." We were still getting water delivery by truck. We had no "utilidor" direct to us.

This created an almost natural barrier between people of the country living without services and those living in comfort. Most of us had larger families than the ones who had come to the north as nurses or teachers.

The "utilidor" became a barrier for a good feeling of community. That was when I was elected to the village council. We did, finally, get water and sewage to the west end of town, but there was a lot of negotiating between the federal and the territorial and the municipal governments.

[Lloyd] *Ellen is philosophical about the Canadian Reindeer Program and its lack of success. It may be a way of life that is too foreign to Inuit.*

[Ellen] *I am looking at it in the long term. I wonder how, in anybody's wildest dreams, did we think that we, in seventy-one years,*

A Sami man, in traditional working clothes, directs activities at a reindeer roundup. A person is not considered to be a real Sami unless they are connected with reindeer.

could make herdsmen out of people who were hunters primarily and trappers secondarily, and who like to live a life that was dictated by the seasons and by what they could get? You were pretty well committed to herding. It had to be your life. It gave you back a lot in return. It gave you food, it gave you shelter, it gave you clothing. It had everything. For Sami it seemed so logical. But then, it took them hundreds of years to learn that lifestyle.

To bring a small group of people into another northern area, another type of lifestyle so foreign to the people who stay in the northern Arctic—it is quite a change you are asking people to make. It was okay when it was government-funded, I think, because in the days when the hunting and trapping was not always good it gave a lot of people a chance to make a living.

It was our life. If you were a Sami and if you were not connected with reindeer, there was something missing from your life. If you were even connected with it on the edge, on the peripheral of it, at least you had contact, you felt it was part of your life.

It is the same way Inuit felt about their hunting and trapping. Hunting came first. But life like that looked chancy. It was chancy on the migration of the caribou. It depended if it was a good year for seals, or whatever. So it was a different lifestyle from herding.

When you are a product of a change of life like that, from one country to another, and you grew up with Sami parents, you are pretty well immersed in the reindeer herding emotionally.

5 Lloyd Binder

Lloyd Binder looks to both sides of his northern heritage for inspiration. As an Inuvaluit he has been a senior manager of economic development for the Northwest Territories, where he urged the development of local resources for the local people. Now he is combining his business skills with his Sami background to develop an economically viable reindeer herding enterprise. Lloyd speaks frankly about the complexities of doing business in today's North.

Lloyd Binder is bottle-feeding two fawns that have been abandoned by their mothers. His herding dog Kix is jealous and also wants attention.

[Lloyd] I was born in Reindeer Station in 1952. Reindeer Station was a thriving little community with upwards of one hundred people at one time. The population included reindeer herders, their extended families, their relatives who were visiting, traders, and the odd bureaucrat who was passing through. As a community grows it needs more and more support personnel. There was also a power plant engineer, a "cat skinner" (Caterpillar tractor operator), and a teacher. But it was unique in the North because it was a closed community that operated entirely as part of the Canadian Reindeer Program. The officials were rather strict about who could live in the town and how long they could stay.

It was a government town. That was probably not a good move from a public

Here a caterpillar tractor leaves Reindeer Station with dozens of reindeer carcasses, the main product in the 1950s. Lloyd is planning to implement meat production in the near future.

relations perspective because it engendered envy and jealousy from people living in other communities and living in the bush. They had misconceptions about the high degree of comfort enjoyed by the people living at Reindeer Station. I suppose that was true of the government officials of the project. But the herders had it a little bit tougher; although, in general, I think that the people associated with the project got the benefit of a certain amount of reindeer meat. They were better off, given that there were no caribou in the area at the time.

When I was growing up in the Mackenzie Delta there was a pretty negative attitude toward Native people—it was not popular to be Native in places such as Inuvik. So, as preteens and teenagers we would dress "White," speak "White," and try not to look too Native. We were somewhat ashamed of our parents, who spoke broken English or English with a heavy accent. It just was not cool. There was a certain amount of shame in being Native.

The water supply for Reindeer Station in the 1950s came from river ice. Lloyd still uses ice for water in his camps, and camp chores include fetching ice or water.

This changed for me when my grandfather took me back to Norway for a visit. I was about eighteen or nineteen. It was a real eye-opener to see the other side of my family, Sami side. In Norway they are considered to be Native, to be the aboriginal people. I found that in northern Norway they were treated the same way as the Native people in northern Canada. There was a real dismissive attitude toward Sami people.

This really stirred something in me. I suddenly thought, "Well I am Sami." And when I came back to Canada, I thought, "Well, by God, I am an Inuvialuit too." That was my turning point. Of course in the 1970s, and even more so in the 1980s, and with the Inuvialuit land claims, the whole environment has changed. People have a real pride in their heritage.

I was discouraged from learning either Samigiella or Inuvialutun. When my mother and father went to school it was forbidden to speak Native languages. My mother and father and

Transportation has always been a major factor in economic development, especially in the Arctic. Here we see a reindeer sleigh, a "Bombadier" tracked vehicle, a dog sled, and a Cessna on skis. Except for the dog sled, Lloyd still uses these forms of transport, along with smaller snowmobiles.

the other students could not speak Inuvialutun at school; they had to speak English. My mother could not speak Samigiella to her brother. At the same time, her parents discouraged the use of Samigiella in public. They would speak the language at home, but if anyone came to visit, my grandmother would say, "Be quiet," and they would switch to English. They did not want to offend anyone's sensibilities. To some extent, Samigiella became a secret language in the family.

My mother and my grandparents also learned Inuvialutun. My mother grew up with both Inuvialutun and Samigiella. My father, of course, grew up speaking Inuvialutun first. He also learned English at an early age. Cyril, his stepfather, was a skilled inter-preter and spoke very good English. But the environment of my parents' youth was one of not speaking your native language.

Our parents decided that us children should not even bother learning Inuvialutun because what damn good was it? You could not speak it anyway. You would get hell if you did. So what was the point? They could not see the benefit to our education since not only could we not use the language, it would get us into trouble at school.

After working many years for the Department of Economic Development and Tourism of the Government of the Northwest Territories, I have become a reindeer herder. We have come full circle with the family, back to the reindeer. The Binder-Pulks had tried to buy into the operation when the herd was privatized in the 1960s. We were not successful. The herd went to Silas Nasigaluak from Tuktoyaktuk, and he was herd owner until 1967 or 1969 when he got sick and decided to sell it. We tried again to buy it, but this time it went to William Nasigaluak, also from Tuktoyaktuk. William operated the herd for two decades or more. When the Inuvialuit Final Agreement (the 1982 Western Arctic land claims settlement) was finalized, Canadian Reindeer Limited, which owned the reindeer, did not negotiate any specific grazing rights with the Inuvialuit. They assumed and insisted that their contract took precedence over the Final Agreement. Well, it did not. So there was a dispute between Canadian Reindeer Limited (CRL) and the Inuvialuit Regional Corporation (IRC). The IRC demanded that CRL pay a grazing fee on the land within the Inuvialuit Settlement Region.

When Canadian Reindeer Limited refused to pay, claiming that they had pre-existing rights, the Inuvialuit sued for nonpayment. Canadian Reindeer Limited, in turn, named Indian and Northern Affairs Canada as a third party. These people were in dispute, with a lot of legal costs and, basically, getting nowhere.

In about 1996, Nellie Cournoyea from the Inuvialuit Regional Corporation and William Nasigaluak from Canadian Reindeer Limited asked me if I would consider forming a new company to buy the reindeer and, in passing, settle the dispute among the three parties. They knew I had a background in business from my

Small groups of tourists and some distant Sami relatives often come to work with the reindeer herd. Lloyd welcomes dude herders and roundup workers.

work with the government. They also knew that I have a long fami-ly history associated with the reindeer.

We have formed a company, the Kunnek Resource Development Corporation, to be the owners of the herd. The major shareholders of this company include my parents, some other individuals, and the Inuvialuit, who collectively hold about one-third of the shares in the company through the Inuvialuit Community Economic Development Organization. I, personally, hold only about one-fifth of the shares. So, it is generally an Inuvialuit-owned and -operated venture. I hope that down the road we get more direct participation from the Inuvialuit.

I began a process, believing it would take of couple of years. I did a very lengthy analysis, economic feasibility and business plan. It took me about two years and I thought I had turned the corner.

Lloyd places notices near the reindeer herd to advise caribou hunters that there are reindeer nearby and not to shoot any. Caribou do stray into the reindeer herd but look different—they are more gray-colored, longer-legged, and wilder. The caribou usually flee when people approach the reindeer herd.

But then the question of environmental impact screening came up with the Inuvialuit Environmental Impact Screening Committee, which had been established under the 1982 Western Arctic claim. Prior to the 1960s, there was a one-page form from the Canadian Department of Indian Affairs and Northern Development that covered all environmental concerns and conditions for oil and gas development. Today, a project of similar size and scope would require a minimum of ten thousand pages of information and associated documentation. These relate especially to the process of meetings, consultations, reviews, and studies of impact statements. It is very rigorous and applies to any economic venture, not just oil and gas. There has been a big change from before claims and after claims, before environmental consciousness and after.

We took a year to do a detailed environmental impact assessment and submitted it for review to the Environmental Screening Committee. This committee reviews the initial environmental impact assessments and determines if the impacts of a project are significant enough to warrant a more extensive review.

Land Agreements in the Mackenzie River Delta

Throughout the history of Canada the federal government has signed treaties with the First Nations. These agreements recognize that First Nations people were here before the Euro-Canadian settlers arrived. In exchange for rights to use the land, the government agreed that First Nations people would be allowed to retain some land, receive cash compensation for surrendering land and rights, and would have special co-management rights in Canada.

Inuit of the Western Arctic have only recently reached an agreement with the federal government. They have been given control over large portions of land in their traditional territory. The governments of Canada and the Northwest Territories have retained control over some of this area and the Gwich'in, in their agreement with the federal government (signed in 1982), also have rights to part of the Mackenzie River Delta area.

Four governments, and many different agencies and departments of each government, have jurisdiction in the area of the reindeer range. Lloyd Binder must consult with all of these authorities whenever he wishes to move his herd, build a corral, or do anything else related to his reindeer. Sometimes it takes longer to get the appropriate approval documents than it does to do the task.

Normally, a herd of four thousand animals will spread out over 1 to 2 miles (1.6 to 3.2 km) as they graze. This herd has been startled and has gathered together.

A good corral design will ensure that the animals can be handled safely and quickly to avoid stress to them. This is the old corral built in the 1930s at Kidluit Bay on Richards Island. Lloyd's new corrals are similar in layout but 18 miles (30 km) to the south.

Unfortunately, the Environmental Screening Committee referred our assessment for a full review by the Environmental Impact Review Board. This required a more detailed Environmental Impact Statement. It took another year to complete this and another year and a half for the review process to be completed.

Some of the rigor of the process was good. But it took an additional two years and probably an additional 50,000 to 75,000 dollars

Lloyd Binder raises reindeer primarily for the antler velvet, which is shipped by air-plane to markets in southern Canada for distribution to Asia.

in hard and soft costs. The review process is targeted at the oil and gas industry, not at agriculture.

Moreover, these rules are being applied to an already existing enterprise. The reindeer have been in northern Canada for over half a century. The system of environmental review is aimed at new developments.

We continually consult with and report to a variety of govern-ment agencies, including federal, territorial and Inuvialuit repre-sentatives within the Inuvialuit Settlement Region Co-Management System which monitor all developments within the Settlement Region. Among these are the Inuvialuit Land Administration, Inuvialuit Game Council, Inuvialuit Hunters and Trappers Committee, the Wildlife Management Advisory Committee for the Northwest Territories, and the Canadian Wildlife Service. And there always seems to be still another organization or committee that has an interest in reindeer.

We report monthly on major occurrences within the industry. Major movements and interaction with wildlife, conflicts with wildlife, or harvesting of wildlife are all significant events. Then we meet annually with the co-managers of the land and the wildlife and report on our overall activities. We report on herd sizes because we have to pay a grazing fee based on the number of reindeer. It is not an onerous system, but there is a fair bit of discipline and rigor to it. Again, this is a new development in the wake of the Land Agreement and the rise of environmentalism.

For example, in the early days, if a herder came across a wolf or a bear, he would kill it to protect his animals. He would probably just leave it, unless he took the hide. Today, if I come across a grizzly bear and kill it, I will have to pay a trophy fee of about $10,000. I have a pretty strong interest in not killing grizzly bears.

When we decided to relocate our corrals from Swimming Point to Skiff Point, where the crossing to the mainland would be easier, we found ourselves caught between two levels of government. Swimming Point is on Inuvialuit community land and Skiff Point is administered by Canada Lands. We had to apply to the federal government to lease the land and for permission to build the new corrals. We also had to consult with the Inuvialuit Land Administration and with the Hunters and Trappers Committee from Tuktoyaktuk. They all put us through a rigorous review process and required that we consult with local communities. All this incurred unexpected costs and unanticipated time.

Our current program has been approved solely for the purpose of caring for the reindeer and harvesting of the antler velvet for medicinal use in the Far East. Technically, we cannot expand our business to host tourists. We would have to obtain a license through an even more difficult review process. Similarly, we are involved with only limited, subsistence meat production. This means we can harvest maybe a half-dozen reindeer each day for a couple of months and sell the meat in the local communities. We must dispose of all the meat, all the offal, and all the hides. There can be nothing left behind. To move beyond this type of cottage

Andrew Gordon, Lloyd's cousin, holds a fawn in preparation for ear tagging and inoculation with Ivomek. The roundup is a very busy time and twenty people or more are needed to care for the animals.

industry would require a great deal of investment. We will have to assess the market before we move ahead.

We would also like to export some of our livestock to other markets. Again, this requires a larger infrastructure than we have right now. There are also many regulations governing such an operation. For now, we capture six or twelve animals and put up a quick screening area among the trees. There we can feed them lichen that we have already picked and convert the reindeer to a hay diet over the course of two months. We then have them certified for export and ship them south.

It is a long haul from Inuvik to other markets such as Calgary. But as long as they can eat, the reindeer should survive the trip in good shape. They are steady grazers and their rumen is constantly working. If they do not eat for twenty-four hours their stomach content liquifies, they get diarrhea, and then you are in trouble. They need to be fed and they need to have low stress levels. So the truck has to be kept quiet. But if you keep it quiet in the truck, have feed, and can manage to let them out every day or two for a couple of hours, a three-day truck ride from Inuvik to Calgary should not be a problem.

Reindeer herding is not something that you can really run well from an office. You can do a certain amount of forecasting and contingency planning, but it is a pretty fluid kind of business with a lot of variables.

6 Cultural Survival in a Global World

Canadian Inuit first met European explorers, whalers, and traders in the sixteenth century. The earliest encounters had little impact on Inuit life. Iron and other new materials were incorporated into the ancient northern lifeways. Whalers may have drawn some people into long-term relationships as Inuit men signed onto crews and the foreigners began living with the local women. In some areas, Inuit began living more or less full-time with the seamen at the temporary whaling stations.

Whaling and other traditional hunting practices, which continue to be important to Inuit, are threatened by global climate changes. In Wainwright, Alaska, researchers from the University of Calgary meet with concerned hunters to map traditional land use and monitor the effects of climate change.

In the traditional Inuit blanket toss, an individual is thrown high in the air. This game expresses the value of individual success, supported by the community.

Traders came for longer periods of time and had a more profound effect. They wanted to exchange European manufactured goods for the fine pelts of the Arctic fox, wolf, polar bear, seal, and other fur-bearing animals. Inuit were already superb hunters and, at first, there was little disruption to their traditional ways of life. Gradually, people relied more and more on the new foods, weapons, and tools. Territories began to center on the trading post, and Inuit economy came to be dominated by the market demands of a foreign country.

In its early days, the young country of Canada paid little attention to the northern reaches of its dominion. The vast, unsettled prairies were awaiting settlement. Gradually, as Canada entered more fully into the global economy, the resources of the North became more important. First, the minerals and forests of the Subarctic were explored and exploited. As communication and transportation systems improved, southerners looked even further north, to the Arctic. Here, the spaces and extremes of climate presented unique challenges to a government wishing to assert its sovereignty. Canada responded by drawing Inuit even closer to the artificial communities focused around the trading establishments. RCMP outposts were built adjacent to the trading posts, and missionaries were encouraged to build churches. Before long, maps of Arctic Canada were dotted with settlements where before there had been only Inuit oral traditions of ancient myths, good hunting spots, and places where their ancestors had lived and laughed.

As Inuit became more tied to settlements they also became less flexible in adapting to ecological changes. When the caribou shifted their annual migration pattern and no longer came near Aklavik in the Mackenzie River Delta, Inuit were left without meat for the winter. Some left their homes and jobs to hunt. The imposed stability of settlement developed from a southern Canadian perspective was challenged. The government reacted by importing reindeer and Sami herders. These, they believed, would provide the predictability and stability required for a "civilized" North.

Lloyd Binder is a product of this attempt to impose a southern view on a northern way of life. His mother, Ellen Pulk Binder, came from Norway when her parents were hired to teach reindeer herding to Inuit of the Western Canadian Arctic. His father, Otto Binder, is an Inuvialuit who has lived in settlements for most of his life. Otto was one of the first Inuit to manage his own reindeer herd. Neither these early efforts, nor later attempts, resulted in a profitable reindeer industry in northern Canada. Too often, regulation and management plans from the south were imposed with little or no regard for the knowledge of the northerners.

In many ways the present struggle to develop a profitable reindeer business reflects tensions in Lloyd's own cultural background. His Sami heritage strives to continue the ancient connection with reindeer. But the traditional cultural values that come from working with reindeer do not preclude using modern technology. When Lloyd calls his friends and

Modern technology is a major part of reindeer herding today. Here, Joh Roland and Lloyd Binder use a global positioning system to plan a traveling route across the tundra.

family from his tundra camps, he uses a cell phone. Travel to and from camps, and out to the herd, is by snowmobile guided by a global positioning system (GPS) rather than by ski with a dog. A laptop computer is used to compose and edit the many reports necessary to keep in business. And Lloyd continually journeys around the circumpolar world on a 737 jet to attend conferences and business meetings with other herders. All of this helps ensure that the reindeer will survive and that the culture of reindeer herding will continue.

In northern Canada, this herding tradition is also challenged by Inuit of the region as they try to preserve their own traditions. The Inuvialuit Final Agreement (or Western Arctic Claim) was settled in 1984. This legal agreement with the Government of Canada describes in detail how the Inuvialuit may participate in the management of renewable and nonrenewable resources in the Western Arctic. Inuit were concerned that the ongoing oil and gas developments would proceed without compensation to the First Peoples of the area. They were also worried that these developments would lead to irreparable ecological damage that would destroy the natural resources and leave Inuit without the means of continuing their hunting traditions. The Final Agreement states the ways in which each level of government can exert control over developments in the Western Arctic.

The Inuvialuit have created two government organizations to respond to development. The Inuvialuit Game Council (IGC) is concerned with renewable resources. It has established the Environmental Impact Screening Committee and the Environmental Impact Review Board to respond to developments that might impact the ecology. The IGC also ensures that the local Hunters and Trappers Committees are kept informed of these developments and have a chance to express any concerns about impacts to their activities.

The Inuvialuit Regional Corporation (IRC) is concerned with financial and commercial issues as it manages the financial compensation that is part of the Final Agreement. Lloyd's reindeer herd operation, as a commercial venture, reports to the IRC. While the IGC monitors and often restricts the herd management activities, the IRC encourages them as an opportunity for economic self-sufficiency.

At the same time that Lloyd's dual background brings tension to his life, it is also the avenue by which these stresses can be resolved. Who in Canada is better prepared by family, education, previous career, and interest to undertake these tasks? His Inuit roots inform the ways in which he consults with elders, works with the various Hunters and Trappers Committees, and meets with Inuit and Euro-Canadian bureaucrats. His Sami background shows him the potential that reindeer offer. Marketing custom-smoked meat, tanned hides, and skin clothing, as well as such cultural tourism events as reindeer sleigh rides, Christmas visits with St. Nicholas, and a stay in a Sami log cabin are all commonplace in Scandinavia. They may well prove to be successful in the Tuktoyaktuk peninsula.

The Challenge of Cultural Survival

The issue of cultural survival affects individuals as much as it impacts on communities. Lloyd may well become a successful reindeer herder. But will his children follow his footsteps and continue the family tradition? While Bernadette, Adam, and Kristian all support their father's efforts, none work on the project. The lure of high wages and an urban lifestyle is outweighing any need to understand their Sami heritage. What will it take to keep the lifestyle alive?

On a more general level, the Inuvialuit of the Western Arctic negotiated the Inuvialuit Final Agreement to preserve their cultural identity and values within a changing northern society. Inuit Circumpolar Conference represents 150,000 Inuit from Alaska, Canada, Greenland, and Chukotka, Russia. It meets every four years to discuss issues of common concern to all these circumpolar people. The goals of the organization are:

- to strengthen unity among Inuit
- to promote Inuit rights at the international level
- to develop Inuit culture and society for the present and the future
- to seek full active participation in the political, economic, and social developments in their homelands
- to develop and encourage long-term policies that safeguard the Arctic environment
- to work for international recognition of the human rights of all indigenous peoples

Cultural survival requires great effort at the individual, community, national, and international level. It also requires that people, governments, and institutions of the world's dominant societies acknowledge the right of other cultures to coexist and to maintain their traditions and beliefs. Our world will be a richer place for the diversity of knowledge, perspective, and understanding.

Resources

Printed Sources

Andrews, Clarence Leroy
1939 *The Eskimo and his reindeer in Alaska.* Caldwell, Idaho: Carsten Printing

Canada
1922 Royal Commission on possibilities of reindeer and musk-ox industries in the Arctic and Sub-arctic regions. Report of the Royal Commission appointed by order-in-council of May 20, 1919, to investigate the possibilities of reindeer and musk-ox industries in the Arctic and Sub-arctic regions of Canada. Ottawa: Government of Canada.

Gaski, Harald (editor)
1997 *Sami culture in a new era. The Norwegian Sami experience.* Seattle: University of Washington Press.

Lomen, Carl J.
1954 *Fifty years in Alaska.* New York: David McKay.

Miller, Max
1935 *The great trek: The story of the five-year drive of a reindeer herd through the icy wastes of Alaska and northwestern Canada.* Garden City, New York: Doubleday Dan.

North, Dick
1991 *Arctic exodus: The last great trail drive.* Toronto: Macmillan of Canada.

Porsild, Alf Erling
1929 *Reindeer grazing in northwest Canada: Report of an investigation of pastoral possibilities in the area from the Alaska-Yukon boundary to the Coppermine river.* Ottawa: F.A. Acland.

Robinson, Michael P. and Karim-Aly S. Kassam
1998 *Sami potatoes. Living with reindeer and perestroika.* Calgary: Bayeux Arts Inc.

Stern, Richard O.
1980 *Eskimos, reindeer and land.* Fairbanks: University of Alaska.

Web Sites

Ministry of Agriculture and Natural Resources: Reindeer Herding
http://www.mmm.fi/english/game/reindeer/

Reindeer Herding in Alaska
http://www.alaskool.org/projects/reindeer/reindeer_ind.htm

Rangifer Research Resources
http://www.dartmouth.edu/~arctic/rangifer/resresources/herding.html

The Challenges of Modern Reindeer Management
http://www.urova.fi/home/renman/eng/index.htm

Human Role in Reindeer and Caribou Systems
http://www.taiga.net/rangifer/

Reindeer Herding in General
http://www.oloft.com/herding.htm

The Arctic Council
http://www.arctic-council.org/index.html

Description of Reindeer in Scandinavia and Northern Russia
http://www.itv.se/boreale/bovts.htm

A History of Reindeer Herding
http://www.paliskunnat.fi/english/poro/historia.htm

Chukotkan Reindeer Herding
http://www.chukotka-ethnography.org/reindeer.html

Explore North: Caribou and Reindeer Links
http://www.explorenorth.com/library/weekly/aa080798b.htm

Memories of a Reindeer Herder
http://www.turtletrack.org/Issues02/Co05182002/CO_05182002_Reindeer.htm

Canadian Polar Information Network
http://www.polarcom.gc.ca

Bering Land Bridge National Preserve: Reindeer and Caribou
http://www.nps.gov/bela/html/rangifer.htm

Index

Photo credits

Frontispiece. Photograph courtesy of the National Archives of Canada, Ottawa PA-212553
Page 2. Map courtesy of Michael P. Robinson.
Page 5. Map courtesy of Bartholomew Ltd.
Page 6. Photograph by L.T. Burwash, 1924, courtesy of the National Archives of Canada, Ottawa PA-99068.
Page 7. Photograph by Richard Harrison, 1949-50, courtesy of the National Archives of Canada, Ottawa PA-114646.
Page 8. Photograph courtesy of Lloyd Binder.
Page 11 top. Photograph courtesy of Glenbow Archives, Calgary NC-1-544.
Page 11 bottom. Photograph courtesy of Glenbow Archives, Calgary NC-1-526c.
Page 12 top. Photograph courtesy of Glenbow Archives, Clagary NC-1-1526.
Page 12 bottom. Photograph courtesy of the National Archives of Canada, Ottawa,PA-130437.
Page 15 top. Photograph courtesy of Glenbow Archives, Calgary NC-1-1170a.
Page 15 bottom. Photograph courtesy of Barbara Godkin.
Page 16. Photograph courtesy of the National Archives of Canada, Ottawa, PA-130444
Page 17. Photograph courtesy of Barbara Godkin.
Page 18. Photograph courtesy Ethnology Collection, Glenbow Museum, Calgary.
Page 19. Photograph courtesy of the National Archives of Canada, Ottawa, PA-121721.
Page 20. Photograph courtesy of Ethnology Collection, Glenbow Museum, Calgary.
Page 23. Photograph courtesy of Lloyd Binder.
Page 24. Photograph by Richard Harrington, 1949-50, courtesy of the National Archives of Canada, Ottawa PA-129923.
Page 25. Photograph courtesy of the National Archives of Canada, Ottawa, PA-145025.
Page 26. Photograph by Richard Harrington, 1952-53, courtesy of the National Archives of Canada, Ottawa PA-129868.
Page 29. Photograph by Mrs. F. McInnis, 1941, courtesy of the National Archives of Canada, Ottawa PA-121720.
Page 30. Photograph by A.E. Porsild, 1934, courtesy of the National Archives of Canada, Ottawa PA-101094.
Page 31. Photograph by J.A. Parsons, 1943, courtesy of the National Archives of Canada, Ottawa PA-135776.
Page 33. Photograph courtesy of Susan B. Peters collection, Glenbow Archives, Calgary.
Page 34. Photograph courtesy of the National Archives of Canada, Ottawa, PA-114667.

Page 35. Photograph courtesy of Lloyd Binder.
Page 36. Photograph courtesy of Lloyd Binder.
Page 37. Photograph courtesy of Lloyd Binder.
Page 38. Photograph courtesy of Barbara Godkin.
Page 42. Photograph by R.S. Finnie, courtesy of the National Archives of Canada, Ottawa PA-130423.
Page 44. Photograph courtesy of the National Archives of Canada, Ottawa PA-101701
Page 46. Photograph by J.A. Parsons, courtesy of the National Archives of Canada, OttawaPA-101108.
Page 48. Photograph courtesy of the Susan B. Peters Collection, Glenbow Archives, Calgary.
Page 50. Photograph courtesy of the Susan B. Peters Collection, Glenbow Archives, Calgary.
Page 51. Photograph courtesy of the Susan B. Peters Collection, Glenbow Archives, Calgary.
Page 52. Photograph courtesy of the Ethnology Collection, Glenbow Museum, Calgary.
Page 54. Photograph courtesy of the Ethnology Collecton, Glenbow Museum, Calgary.
Page 56. Photograph Courtesy of Lloyd Binder.
Page 57 top. Photograph courtesy of the Susan B. Peters collection, Glenbow Archives, Calgary.
Page 58. Photograph courtesy of the Susan B. Peters collection, Glenbow Archives, Calgary.
Page 59. Photograph courtesy of Susan B. Peters collection, Glenbow Archives, Calgary.
Page 61. Photograph courtesy of Lloyd Binder.
Page 62. Photograph courtesy of Lloyd Binder.
Page 63. Photograph courtesy of Lloyd Binder.
Page 64. Photograph courtesy of the National Archives of Canada PA-500036.
Page 65. Photograph courtesy of Lloyd Binder.
Page 67. Photograph courtesy of Lloyd Binder.
Page 69. Photograph courtesy of Karim-Aly Kassam, University of Calgary.
Page 70. Photograph courtesy of Karim-Aly Kassam, University of Calgary.
Page 72. Photograph courtesy of Lloyd Binder.

Colour Insert.
Page 1. Courtesy of Lloyd Binder.
Page 2 left. Courtesy of Lloyd Binder.
Page 2 top right. Courtesy of Lloyd Binder.
Page 2 bottom right. Courtesy of Lloyd Binder
Page 3 top right. Courtesy of Lloyd Binder.
Page 3 bottom right. Courtesy of Lloyd Binder.
Page 4 top left. Courtesy of Lloyd Binder.
Page 4 bottom left. Courtesy of Barbara Godkin.
Page 4 top right. Courtesy of Lloyd Binder.
Page 4 bottom right. Courtesy of Glenbow Museum, Calgary.